GUIDEPOST

TO

MARRIAGE

BY

DR. BRENDA A. HOLMES THOMAS

Guidepost to Marriage, true story

All rights reserved. No part of this publication may be reproduced, stored in a retrieval system, or transmitted in any form or by any means, electronic, mechanical, photocopying, recording, or otherwise without the prior permission of the author Dr. Brenda A. Holmes Thomas, by the provisions of the Copyright, Designs and Patents Act 1988 or under the terms of any license permitting limited copying issued by the Copyright Licensing Agency. For permission requests, write to the copyright holder at brendathomas.2015@gmail.com, and use the subject line: Permission to Reproduce. Address your request "GUIDEPOST TO MARRIAGE, true story":

Junkanoo Publications is a professional publishing division of Junk@Noo Consulting LLC.

www.junkanoopublications.com

Valdosta, GA

ISBN: 979-8-9927152-9-3 (Paperback)

I dedicate this book to the Lord,

who gave me the vision and the assignment.

After coming off a church fast in 2009, God placed on my heart to write three books, each one carrying purpose, healing, and truth. Guidepost to Marriage, true story (2009), Escape, Not Without Scars (2014), Fourteen Tiny, Big Footprints (2016).

This work is an act of obedience and faith, a reflection of His guidance throughout my journey.

To God be the glory for every word written.

Acknowledgements

Special acknowledgment to the following: Joan P. Cobb, Joshua and Jalisha Lambert, David While, Jeremy Rodgers, Veronica Graydon, Thermond Howard Jr., Vera C. Phillips, Annie K. Robinson, Carolyn McIntyre Hardy, Teresa Taylor, Linda D. Corbett, Michelle Holland, Miriam Warren, Kimbely Speed, James Hatch, Orynthia Gaines Hahira, LaVito and Sheena Holmes, Tiffani and Curtis Wright, Emma Green, LaKatilin Wright, Bernice and David Washington, Ruth Wright, Nichole Corbett, Darrell and Patricia Barron, Mary and Odessa Murphy, Albert and Ellen Ann Burns, Sharon Garvin, Timeka Cosley, Nia and Khristian Sr., Neal Hester Jr, L'Marquis and Jasmine Holmes, Robert Morris, Mary Manson, Ronald L. Fann Sr., Chantel Pridgon, Stephanie Morrow, Lovecia and Dessie Oglesby, Kathryn Phillips, Angelia and Henry T. Wright, Reginal and Shirley Phillips, Candice Thomas, Sheila & Ronaldo Fann, Betty C. Thomas, Jean M. Christie, Gerry and Ina Davis, Guy Kwame, Carla Brooks, Denise Allen, Ishmael Rodgers, Tina White, Albert Taylor II, Quincy Holmes, Peggy Booth, Bridgette Carter, Donyelle Moore Macomb, Elizabeth Taylor, Aaron Slydell, Ambrose B. King, Jr., Johnny and Ruby Wolfe, Deborah L Demps, Chryl Raye, Gail Tyson, Maggie Preston Raymond, Cheryl Davis, Kara Davis, Andre Davis, Rose Waller, Solomon and Sharon Nixon Jr., Darrell Allen, Todd and Vanessa Ennis, Otis Greene, Vivian P. Harris, William L Poole, Marie Pettiford, Sidney and Barbara Sue Johnson.

TABLE OF CONTENTS

INTRODUCTION

God created all kinds of creatures and animals. Then he created the man, Adam, who did not have a mate. God put the man to sleep and created a female for the man, Adam, and he called her Eve.

God ordained marriage when the world was created. "And the Lord God said, It is not good that the man should be alone; I will make him an help meet (mate) for him" (Genesis 2:18). "And the Lord God caused a deep sleep to fall upon Adam, and he slept: and he took one of his rib, and closed up the flesh instead thereof" (Genesis 2:21); "And the rib, which the Lord God had taken from man, made he a woman, and brought her unto the man" (Genesis 2:22). "And Adam said, This is now bone of my bones, and flesh of my flesh: she shall be called Woman, because she was taken out of man" (Genesis 2:23).

Here, you will find information to help guide and direct you through a successful marriage. If you follow the guidepost examples throughout the word of God, you cannot go wrong. There is a right way you can follow and there is a wrong way.

However, you should take the correct path. "There is a way that seemeth right unto a man, but the end thereof are the ways of death" (Proverbs 16:25).

In this book, *Guidepost to Marriage*, there will be many examples of people's lives. The names will be changed to protect their identity. Their stories will be told, and through God's word, they will find the answer to the different situations that are happening in their lives. The information will be explained through the word of God, and there will be a response to each story's circumstances. A biblical point of view will be given to each story by using the word of God on what should have happened or what did not happen in their marriage. Steps will be given on how to have a successful marriage and how to commit to becoming one flesh through the covenant you made with God.

CHRISTAIN AND NONCHRISTAIN MARRIAGE

Unfortunately, the divorce rate is just as high in the Christian communities as in the world. This should not be. God has given a guideline for each Christian to follow. The guide for Christian couples is written in the Holy Bible. There are several places in the Bible for God's followers to follow concerning marriage; it is imperative for Christian couples to find them so they can enlighten their relationship with God's will. Likewise, when you accept Jesus as savior, you should follow and obey his word instead of your petty wants and whims. "Trust in the Lord with all thine heart; and lean not unto thine own understanding" (Proverbs 3:5). "In all thy ways acknowledge him, and he shall direct thy paths" (Proverbs 3:6).

The guidepost God set for all of us to follow is always available to everyone at any time. A married couple must be willing to submit to each other. They cannot go by what they feel, but by what the word of God says they should be doing for each other.

For example, you may want to raise your children the way your parents raised you. However, your wife may know another way of rearing children, therefore, both of you must compromise. It is crucial that you understand that it is your decision about how you raise your children and not your parents. As the word of God said, (Genesis 2: 24), "Therefore shall a man leave his father and his mother, and shall cleave unto his wife: and they shall be one flesh."

Also, your parents might not approve of your spouse, but you must stand by his or her side, for it's your spouse and not theirs. I was told by, Angel, a woman I met a few years back, that her mother in-law told her husband to leave her because she believed Angel was trying to kill him. Angel's mother in-law told Angel repeatedly that she was trying to kill her son. Angel loved her husband unconditionally. She was very hurt that her mother in-law would think of her in that manner, so much that, she went into deep depression until her faith in God brought her out of the depression. Sadly, Angel's cowardly husband moved out of the house and left Angel.

In this case, the husband should have stayed with his wife. The Lord said "Wherefore they are no more twain, but one flesh. What therefore God hath joined together, let not man put asunder" (Matthew 19:6). God said in James 3:8; James 3:9; James 3:10, "But the tongue can no man tame; it is an unruly evil, full of deadly poison." "Therewith bless we God, even the Father; and therewith curse we men, which are made after the similitude of God." "Out of the same mouth proceedeth blessing and cursing. My brethren, these things ought not so to be." It is important to watch what you say about couples unless God has given you a word of knowledge or wisdom to reveal about a situation in someone's marriage. We are to be led by the spirit and speak of what we do know for a fact and not what we think or feel about a situation.

In fact, this happened to me; one time my child's friend's mother came to pick up my daughter to take her to a party. I was married into a blended family with other daughters, but their dad refused to let them go to the party. We had a slight argument where voices were raised with him at one point stating, "I thought you were raising debutantes not whores." The mother of the friend had a family emergency so she could not bring my daughter home. Husband and wife should be careful what they say about other people. "But the tongue can no man tame; it is an unruly evil, full of deadly poison" (James 3:8). Maybe one of you could take your child to the party or talk to the host's parents. Just find a solution that satisfies both of you civilly, for marriage is no place for kiddy arguments.

In addition, Angel's husband should have stayed with her, and he should not have followed his mother's opinion. Angel was his wife; he should have loved her enough to stay and talk everything over with her, but instead, he moved out of the house. It made Angel believe that he agreed with his mother's opinion of his wife. James 1:8 says, "A double-minded man is unstable in all his ways. Submit yourselves therefore to God. Resist the devil, and he will flee from you" (James 4:7).

Another example is that your child may want to go out with a friend to a party, and your spouse does not agree. Perhaps he or she was not raised with a girl going out after a certain time of night. You need to understand their view of the situation and compromise. So, she called and asked me could my daughter spend the night at her house. I gave permission to let my daughter spend the night. It caused a huge riff in our relationship because we were torn between viewpoints in raising children. In fact, we were not the same for months; this could all have been resolved if we talked properly about it like adults prior to this incident. Of course, we had no way of knowing how this would turn out. But that is why I wrote this book, so mistakes like this one would not occur to other Christian couples' marriages. Therefore, in situations concerning our children, we must come together, discuss, and make decisions on how we are going to handle raising our children. In fact, we should establish rules for the family and how we want to raise our children before we get married.

Pork in Beans and Pomegranate met while in college. Pork in Beans went to a different college. Pomegranate finished college and they got married. They were married for 40 years. To their union, they had three children. Pork in Beans truly loved Pomegranate the way Jesus loved the church. They shared a great example of how to show true love. We all make mistakes in life. Whenever we went to their home, they always seemed happy with each other. I am sure they had disagreements about things because Pork in Beans was very competitive and smart. Pomegranate was a highly intelligent woman. But they seemed to talk everything out.

The Bible says in Ephesians 4:26, "Be ye angry, and sin not: let not the sun go down upon your wrath". You should make up with your wife or husband before going to sleep.

Pork in Beans did a lot of drinking in his early years of life. He ended up having many health issues, but Pomegranate never left his side. She continued to nurse him and stayed by his side. He got better, and they traveled around the country. They had so much fun, laughing, talking, and moving around seeing different places.

The couple followed the Bible's way though their life. Pork in Beans and Pomegranate stayed together 40 years until his death. She said she had forty wonder full years of marriage to Pork in Beans; he smiled and gave up the ghost and died.

Pomegranate continued to live her life alone. She was very happy and content with living life everyday with joy and happiness. Pomegranate had some sick days, but God brought her through. God will never leave you nor forsake you; he will be with you until the end of time. The Bible says in Hebrews 13:5, "Let your conversation be without covetousness; and be content with such things as ye have: for he hath said, I will never leave thee, nor forsake thee".

LOVE

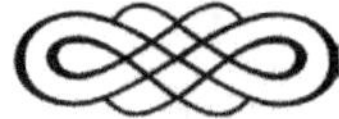

Husbands, love your wives, even as Christ also loved the church, and gave himself for it" (Ephesians 5:25). Colossians 3:19, Husbands, love your wives, and be not bitter against them. Christ loved mankind so much that he died for us. He never hesitated to die for us; therefore, there is no greater love than to lay down your life for a friend.

Buddy and Strawberry met in second grade; it was love at first sight. Strawberry had a boyfriend in fourth grade. She started dating Buddy in ninth grade, and they eventually got married. They have been married for 51 years. Buddy loved his wife with such passion that he did everything in his power to satisfy her every need. He loved his wife Strawberry, with such an explosion of passion that it lit up the morning sky. The sweet love that they shared was magnificent, and it radiated when they walked across the room. As they walked across the room, the stars would shine brighter. The romance was great because they were full of love and passion. Buddy and Strawberry, in their old age, still loved each other. People around them could see the love they shared together.

It was such a joy to see love between couples that continue to love each other as Christ loves the church. "So ought men to love their wives as their own bodies. He that loveth his wife loveth himself" (Ephesians 5:28).

Peaches loved her husband, Phil, with such intensity that she did everything in her power to please him. When Phil decided he wanted to go to medical school to become a doctor, Peaches supported Phil by working extra shifts to pay for his schooling and put off her dreams of having kids at that period in her life so they could afford Phil's dream. Peaches was like the virtuous women in the Bible, remaining or standing by her man, no matter what situations she was put through. When you love your wife and treat her with kindness and like she is the best thing ever happened to you, after Jesus, she will stand by you through the hard times and the good times of life. It is important for wives to submit to their own husband. The Bible said, "Wives, submit yourselves unto your own husbands, as it is fit in the Lord" (Colossians 3:18).

Peaches loved Phil and was there for him through everything he needed. He was there for her when they decided to have a child. After the first child, he did not want her to have any more children. The word says be fruit and multiply and Peaches wanted to have more children. "And God blessed Noah and his sons, and said unto them, Be fruitful, and multiply, and replenish the earth" (Genesis 9:1). She had two more children and he divorced Peaches. The divorce took a toll on Peaches and Phil married her best friend. Peaches never really recovered from what happened to her, but her faith in God carried her through the hard times. She raised her three children alone. She did not ever marry again.

Blake and Joan have been married for 55 years. They met at a convention, and they were very much attracted to each other. They talked and laughed at the convention and went out to dinner while in New Jersey. While out for dinner, they discovered through conversation they had similar interests in plays, spiritual things, business affairs, and family. They grew up with different family backgrounds. He was born and raised in the city, and she was born in a small town. She was a dedicated teacher, and he was a businessman. Blake and Joan were working in different places. They wanted to be together; after a short courtship of four months, Blake asked Joan to marry him. They fell in love with each other. Blake and Joan courted for four more months. After eight months, they got married. Blake and Joan are happily married after 55 years. They both have such a glow on their faces when you meet them. They both offer encouraging words, reminding us that love holds the key to keeping your marriage together. The Bible says, "And above all things have fervent charity among yourselves: for charity shall cover the multitude of sins" (1 Peter 4:8). When you love each other, love hides your faults. You are to walk in love each day of your lives. "Use hospitality one to another without grudging" (1 Peter 4:9). Marriage doesn't need murmuring and complaining, it needs communication and compromise with each other. "For it is God which worketh in you both to will and to do of his good pleasure." "Do all things without murmurings and disputings" (Philippians 2:13-14).

One summer morning, Apricot was taking a stroll around the pond. She was thinking to herself, "What a lovely morning!" The bird were chirping and the crickets were singing. The frogs were making ribbit, ribbit sounds. You could even hear the sounds of a train.

Apricot looked up and saw a man standing at the pond. She was a little startled to see him. He appeared to be a handsome man with black hair and a distinguished face. His face radiated from the beginning of a new morning while standing in front of the pond. Apricot was strolling slowly toward the side of the pond where the young man was standing. As she moved closer to him, she realized he was someone she had seen before at a beach party, but she did not know him. Bean and Apricot met and had a conversation with each other, and they decided to go out on a date. They went on several dates and decided to get married.

They had a small wedding; it was held in Florida. They were so much in love with each other. Bean and Apricot had a short honeymoon in the Bahamas. While married, Bean went into the military. Bean and Apricot had four children. They raised the children in Florida until they became adults.

Bean loved to play with his grandchildren. He also loved to play with the neighborhood children. Bean had different kinds of games for children to play with at his home. He loved all people in the world. Bean loved his neighbors and did not wrong anyone. "Be not a witness against thy neighbor without cause; and deceive not with thy lips" (Proverbs 24:28). Apricot loved her neighbor too, but she was not as friendly as her husband.

Bean and Apricot's marriage was built on character and love. "Through wisdom is a house builded; and by understanding it is established: A wise man is strong; yea, a man of knowledge increaseth strength" (Proverbs 24: 3, 5). Bean and Apricot lived and followed the word of God.

Bean and Apricot were happily married for 49 years. They shared a beautiful life together. Bean and Apricot stayed together until his death at the age of seventy. She lived many years after his death. "Every word of God is pure: he is a shield unto them that put their trust in him" (Proverbs 10: 5).

While strolling through the garden, Lemon saw the most beautiful flowers. Lemon also met the handsome man named Corn walking in the garden with the butterflies of all colors flying around in the garden. The sun shined on the dessert garden; it splintered rays of prism filled light that beautified the garden. Such a beautiful day in the garden, the sky illuminated the flowers showing many colors. Lemon looked at Corn as the most handsome man she ever saw in her life. Lemon was so amazed to see a handsome man glowing looking at her; she was so shy and did not know what to say. Corn spoke to Lemon and asked her to have a glass of lemonade while they talked to each other. After talking to each other, they decided to continue to see each other.

Corn and Lemon were Christians so they did group dating. They went out with their church friends as couples. They all went to church together. They also attended church functions together. As they continued to date, Corn asked Lemon to marry him. Lemon said yes to Corn's proposal. They both were so happy about getting married; they really love each other.

Corn was such a calm spirited man and very friendly to all people. He did not meet any strangers. Corn remembered people by name. Adults and children loved him. Lemon loved him very much. Lemon was a quiet person and a very nice lady.

Corn was in the air force as a pilot. He was shot down during the war, but he did not get hurt. Some people hid him from our enemy. God was merciful and with him during those hard times.

Lemon was home waiting on him. When he returned home, they got married. To their union, they had two children, a boy and a girl. Corn became a pastor and started a church out of a home. His church grew into a big church, and he was a pastor for many years.

Corn really loved his wife. He supported his wife and children. In his younger days, he showed love to Lemon. Corn loved Lemon and the Bible says, "Husbands, love your wives, even as Christ also loved the church, and gave himself for it" (Ephesians 5:25). Corn and Lemon were married for 63 years. Corn died, but Lemon still loved him even in death. They had a blessed marriage and lived many wonderful years together.

FORGIVING YOUR MATE

"Husbands, love your wives, and be not bitter against them" (Colossians 3:19). A marriage that lasted 63 years and 7 months until death separated them. The lady of this couple was crippled, and the man was very handsome. Apple and Bud worked together in the field picking cotton. The sun shining on Bud's handsome face attracted Apple to him. Apple had low self-esteem and she didn't think she was pretty. Apple fell out of a tree when she was 13-years old, and they did not have x-rays during that time, so her hip bone rubbed away. This is what caused her to become crippled. She had such a beautiful personality, smiled a lot and served people. Apple had strong faith in God and she always read her Bible. While working in the field one day, Apple asked Bud to marry her, and he said yes. She was very surprised that Bud said yes because of her low self-esteem. Bud was a man that lived by his word was his bond. He kept his word and on December 12, 1928, they got married.

After they got married, they did not have children for four years. It seemed as though they were not going to be able to have children, but Apple got pregnant with a daughter. The baby was born, but she died a few days later. Apple kept her faith in God; she believed that whatever is to be, is going to be. Maybe a year later, Apple got pregnant again with another daughter. This daughter lived and she had two other children. Bud worked very hard to provide for his family. He loved his children, but Bud had not given his life to God. He went to church, but he was not saved. Bud started cheating on his wife and living a wild life. Apple loved Bud and she had no intention of leaving him. She often said he takes good care of his children and family. She put him in God's hands, still believing whatever is going to be, will be. She did not worry about the situation; she just kept her faith in God. Bud was committing adultery. Apple cooked for Bud every day because he could not boil water. He depended on his wife to take care of him and the children. They had a nice home to raise their children in and he was the provider. Apple did what the Bible say, "Forbearing one another, and forgiving one another, if any man have a quarrel against any: even as Christ forgave you, so also do ye" (Colossians 3:13). Apple forgave Bud and was going to stay married to him.

When Bud reached forty, a bale of cotton fell on his neck and his neck was broken. Bud thought he was going to die. After this experience, he had an encounter with Jesus. He lived for forty more years. Jesus turned Bud's life around; he served the people, he was a giver, a good husband, and neighbor. Bud became a deacon in his church and served his fellow man. Everyone loved Bud and Apple in their community. He repented and turned his life around and served God until he died. Apple lived eight years after Bud died. Apple said, "Forgive and love will prevail". "Casting all your care upon him: for he careth for you" (1 Peter 5:7). God knows what is best for you and your family.

Ben skipped school one day and came to Angel's middle school when she was in the 7th grade. He saw Angel and tried to talk to her, but Angel was afraid of boys. She also was a tom boy and did not like boys. When Ben saw her, he ran after Angel, but she could run very fast and he could not catch her. Angel ran back into the school. Angel was outside for recess at the time when Ben saw her and chased after her. He liked her at first sight. Ben was in the 9th grade.

One more year had passed and Angel was going to the same school as Ben. He saw her again, but at that time, he had a girlfriend. Angel still did not like boys in 8th grade. She was a homely looking girl with low self-esteem. Angel wore her hair in ball up on top of her head. She wore long dresses and bobby socks. Angel did not iron her clothes, so she was also wrinkled every day at school. However, she looked like a mess, but she still had a few friends. She mostly spent her time with her cousins.

The next year in 9th grade, Angel's cousin started fixing her hair, and she dressed better. This was her Cinderella moment; she started wearing pants and had a beautiful shape under all those big, wrinkled clothes. One day, she went to the teen center which was down the street from her home. Ben came to the teen center and saw Angel, but he did not know who she was at that time. He asked someone who was that girl and someone told him. He walked over to see her, but he could not believe it was her. Ben still had a girlfriend, but he still liked Angel from the first time he saw her at middle school.

Finally, he broke up with his girlfriend. Ben tried to talk to Angel at school, but he was a poplar boy, and she did not trust him. Her stepdad went to the same church Ben attended so he knew him. He asked her stepdad if he could come to their home to date her and he told him yes. Her stepdad told Ben the rules he had to follow to date her. He had a ten o'clock curfew to leave their home. Ben really respected her and he put Angel on a pedestal. He did not let anything happen to Angel; he protected her from the world. Angel was a very naive girl and sheltered from the world. Ben was a very funny boy, and he was loved by most people. He made friends very easily wherever he went in the world. Ben was a very likable person it was very hard to stay angry with.

Ben and Angel attended college together for a while, and Ben decided to go back into the army. Ben was in the Marines on his first tour in the military. Angel continued to attend college, and they got married her junior year. Angel was 19-years old when she married her first loved, Ben. She believed that she and Ben would be together until death do them apart. They spent 14 years of their lives together. Angel and Ben spent their time traveling around the world. They had lots of fun, meeting new people and making friends. Ben and Angel enjoyed spending time with each other. Unfortunately, Angel was not enough for Ben. He needed extramarital affairs in his life, and he discovered that one woman was not enough for him. Ben had a hearty appetite for other women. This was a sex addiction for Ben. He could not get enough of other women. Angel did not leave him because she believed in staying married. In spite of his addiction for other women, Angel and Ben started having children at the ages 23 and 25. A preacher said he could not help them because Ben did not want to give up his addiction of other women; he decided this during counseling sessions.

If there was a function or program they were to attend as a couple, he would tell Angel to get a babysitter. If she could not get one, she would have to stay home with the child. Ben was the person who wanted children, but Angel had to raise them basically alone. Ben was all about himself and the other ladies. He did not take fatherhood seriously. He wanted children because his mother would ask, "When are you going to have children"? She thought Angel could not have children, but she was not trying to get pregnant from Ben because she did not feel he was ready for a family, maturity wise, and he was still being unfaithful to her. Often older parents felt you were supposed to have children; it did not matter whether you were ready to have children or to be parents.

Ben would go to the functions and programs alone like he had no responsibilities. If Angel went to the function with him, he would leave her at a table and spend the whole time with other people. Then he would come and get Angle when it was time to go home. Being with other women caused problems in their marriage; Ben was an adulterer. Ben told Angel that he found the love of his life and he wanted to get married again. Angel finally gave up and got a divorce. That destroyed her confidence in marriage. She was devastated because she believed so much in being married until death do you apart. After 14 years, she decided to try marriage again. Angel forgave Ben for everything he ever did to her. She loves him in Christ today and would do anything she could to help if he needed her to. According to Ephesians 3:2-3-7, "With all lowliness and meekness, with longsuffering, forbearing one another in love;" "Endeavouring to keep the unity of the Spirit in the bond of peace." "But unto every one of us is given grace according to the measure of the gift of Christ."

Six years later, Angel met Bobo and ten years after that, she married him. "Be sober, be vigilant; because your adversary the devil, as a roaring lion, walketh about, seeking whom he may devour:" (1 Peter 5:8). Angel and Bobo loved each other with such intensity and excitement when they met and came in contact with each other. When they walked in a room and saw each other, the room lit up as if it had 1,000 candles burning around the room. Angel just looked at him with delight when he entered the room, and you could see the love in her eyes for him; just like a flower opens up when the bees pollinate it. Bobo's broad shoulders and his straight walk like a soldier lit Angel's passion for him. It seemed as though they had the same heartbeat. Angel wanted to be submitted to Bobo with all her heart and no other man. "Submitting yourselves one to another in the fear of God" (Ephesians 5:21-28). "So ought men to love their wives as their own bodies. He that loveth his wife loveth himself." It appeared at one time that there was so much love between Bobo and Angel. But Angel was deceived by Bobo. He left her for another woman and moved out of their home. Bobo became an adulterer; he said he wanted something "Hot!" Angel still did not really know what happened to their marriage. It seemed to be lots of little simple things that did not make any sense to her and could have been resolved easily if they really had talked about the things with an open mind. For example, refusing to get the stepson's ears pierced and pay for it. The second reason was Angel worked for the summer on purpose to save money to buy her son a car. Angel's daughter and her boyfriend found a truck in her price range for $1,700; that was a God send, because the truck lasted her son 8 years, contrary to what Bobo thought, her belief, but he could have had it done himself. Angel still loved her husband and they both decided not to get a divorce. The Bible says, "Put on the whole armour of God, that ye may be able to stand against the wiles of the devil" "For we wrestle not against flesh and blood, but against principalities, against powers, against the rulers of the darkness of this world, against spiritual wickedness in high places" (Ephesians 6:11-12). Angel chose to forgive Bobo and there was no bitterness against him or the young lady. Bobo allowed the wiles of the devil to deceive him. Angel prayed that he would repent and turn his life around. Bobo said he did not want to lose his soul and miss seeing and spending eternal life with Jesus. This world will pass away and nothing on this earth will matter but being right with Jesus. One day, we all must leave this world to go home with Jesus. To gain this whole world and lose your soul, nothing in this world is worth your soul. You can surrender all your hurts, anger and disappointments to Jesus. He loves the brokenhearted and Jesus will heal your heart from hurts. Therefore, turn everything over to Jesus and he will make everything alright. Jesus is the truth and the light; you must go through him to be set free of all your addictions. Nothing is impossible to overcome with God in this short walk through life's journey. "That Christ may dwell in your heart by faith; that ye, being rooted and grounded in love, "May be able to comprehend with all saints what is the breadth, and length, and depth, and height; "And to know the love of Christ, which passeth knowledge, that ye might be filled with all the fullness of God" (Ephesians 3:17-19). Jesus has already died for us, and we are justified in Christ no matter what sin we have committed except the one sin you cannot get forgiveness for. We are the righteousness of God through Jesus Christ. We must all repent and turn away from our sins. He will forgive us, but we must stop doing that which is wrong. "There hath no temptation taken you but such as is common to man: but God is faithful, who will not suffer you to be tempted above that ye are able; but will with the temptation also make a way to escape, that ye may be able to bear it" (1 Corinthians 10:13). Bobo could not escape living in sin with the other women. He chose to live an adulteress life instead of following the will of God. God is just and He gives people free will to follow him or not. "For the Son of man is come to save that which was lost" (Matthew 18:11). Angel still had to forgive Bobo; the Bible says, in Matthew 18:21-22, "Then came Peter to him, and said, Lord, how often shall my brother sin against me, and I forgive him? Till seven times? Jesus saith unto him, I say not unto thee, Until seven times: but, Until seventy times seven."

Let's take a look at another situation on forgiveness. Grapes and Slick met about eleven years ago at a big store in the city. Slick was handsome and he knew how to manipulate women, having them eating out of his hands and wrapped around his finger. Grapes did not know what hit her; the lies he told were electric and believable. She tried to resist him, and she did not want to give in to her attraction for him. But his words charmed her and were too overwhelming and powerful for her to resist. The Bible tells us, "Submit yourselves therefore to God. Resist the devil, and he will flee from you" (James 4:7).

James, 3:8-10, "But the tongue can no man tame; it is an unruly evil, full of deadly poison." "Out of the same mouth proceedeth blessing and cursing. My brethren, these things ought not so to be." Slick and Grapes dated for two and a half years and then they got married. They had a daughter and a son together. He wooed Grapes off her feet, and they lived happily for about three years. He helped support his family and paid half of the bills. After three years, Slick turned against his wife and stopped taking care of his children. It seemed that he turned against his children based on what he felt about his wife. "Husbands, love your wives, and be not bitter against them." "Fathers, provoke not your children to anger, lest they be discouraged." "But he that doeth wrong shall receive for the wrong which he hath done: and there is no respect of persons" (Colossians 3:19-21-25). Slick committed adultery on

Grapes multiple times. Other women came to their house because he told them he was not married. One woman followed him home and came back the next morning while he was at work. She told everyone and revealed that her mother did not trust her husband, so she followed him home. After that, Slick stayed with the woman in the hotel in another town. In addition, he committed adultery with the woman who worked at the cable place. Slick kept prophylactic in his car and in the home closet. He did not think his wife would find them in the house or car. He did not use the prophylactic on his wife.

He ran women like a herd of cattle. Slick was with one woman today and he changed to another one the next day. It appeared that he had a low image of himself that he needed a multitude of women to satisfy him. But he was still not fulfilled nor satisfied with his life. It did not matter what Grapes felt, thought or did for him. It was just not enough to satisfy him. Slick had an enormous appetite for a variety of women; his wife was not able to compete. He did not know how to love or show real love to his wife. He needed to love his wife as Christ loves the church.

Grapes did not love Slick anymore because he hurt her heart deeply many times. Slick was a big liar. He did not help take care of the children. But God requires us to forgive everyone. She needed to forgive Slick. She needed to stop being angry with her husband, reconcile and forgive him since he still lived in the home. Grapes did not want him. He stayed in the same house, but he slept in a different room. The Bible says in Ephesians 4:26-27-31-

32, "Be ye angry, and sin not: let not the sun go down upon your wrath: "Neither give place to the devil". "Let all bitterness, and wrath, and anger, and clamor, and evil speaking, be put away from you, with all malice". "And be ye kind one to another, tenderhearted, forgiving one another, even as God for Christ's sake hath forgiven you".

It was a summer day when the ocean breeze was blowing the hair of Plum back and forth like a world wind while she laid with her body to the sun. Her body shined like a candle in the dark. The sparkles from her shiny body caught his attention. As he ran past her with the beach sand popping up behind him, the sparkle from her body magnetized his eyes in Plum's direction. He jogged over to her and said, "You're a beautiful woman who radiates my eyes; that pulled me into your direction." String Bean introduced himself to Plum. "I am String Bean. Your beauty has captured my attention. I could not resist meeting you." Plum was a little stunned by his approach, but she did not run away from him; she stayed and listened to String Bean's sweet talk. Then she said, "I am Plum." She started to give him a false name, but after listening to him she changed her mind.

Plum was sunbathing while reading a book. String Bean was jogging on the beach. Plum put her book down when String bean approached her. He asked her to go to the beach party that was going to be held on the beach that night. The beach party was to watch the 400-hundred-pound turtles come in from the sea to lay their eggs on the beach. The scientists were monitoring the turtles.

They had music, food, and drinks at the beach party. They agreed to meet back at the beach at seven o'clock. They were on vacation for a week.

After a week vacation, String Bean and Plum continued to see each other. They dated for about one year. They went to a family reunion in Florida. String Bean and Plum enjoyed the trip to the family reunion. While at the family reunion, String Bean asked Plum to marry him. Plum said yes to String Bean's proposal.

Then they returned home from the family reunion. After a month, they went to the courthouse and got married. String Bean and Plum had one child, a son. String Bean and Plum were very hard workers. They worked all their adult lives. They were married 41 years.

String Bean loved Plum, but there were some problems with drinking alcohol. Plum had a greater problem consuming alcohol. String Bean had a problem; he had a mean streak in him, and he fought his wife occasionally. String Bean and Plum were overcomers, and they recommitted their lives to God. Therefore, they were delivered from their faults and became new people in Christ Jesus.

String Bean and Plum turned a new leaf in their marriage. And He said, "The things which are impossible with men are possible with God" (Luke 18:27). If String Bean and Plum stayed on the Lord's side, they would be fine in Christ. Therefore, if any man be in Christ, he is a new creature: old things are passed away; behold, all things are become new" (1 Corinthians 5:17).

LOVE AND ENDURANCE

Tomato and Pear met in college and they fell in love. He and she were both great basketball players. Tomato went overseas to play ball for many years. They did not have contact with each other for many years. Tomato was unfaithful and got another young lady pregnant. Even though he sinned, he did the right thing and married his baby's mother. They had other children to this union. He did everything to make his marriage great like the vows he had made to his wife. He stayed married for many years, but his heart ached secretly for his first love. Although his heart ached for Pear, he stayed committed to his marriage.

Life was sad for Pear, but she finished college. She got a job and started working. Also, she started living her life again. The road was not easy, but she persevered towards her destiny. She had to go on without him. She had been raised to have faith in God, and taught that He orders your footsteps. She dated again but never got married.

After many years, Tomato's marriage failed and they got a divorce. His love for Pear never left from in the back of his mind.

He did not know where to find Pear nor did he know whether she was married or not. He did not know where to look for her because it had been many years since they'd met in college. He had been gone from this country for many years and he lived abroad.

When Tomato came back to the States, he went to Atlanta to live, and then he moved back to his hometown where he was raised. Tomato was surprised; he found out Pear was working and living in Atlanta. He made contact with her and they talked. He made his affection known to her, and they got back together. Later on, they got married. They had a church wedding. Pear moved to his hometown and quit her job. Tomato was very happy to find Pear again. They loved each other and their love grew stronger each day.

To their union, Tomato and Pear had three children. They loss two babies after they were born. One baby lived for many hours, and the other, a few days. The last baby made it all the way with God's purpose for the baby's life. "He is ever merciful, and lendeth; and his seed is blessed" (Psalm 38:26). "Trust in the Lord with all thine heart; and lean not unto thine own understanding. In all thy ways, acknowledge him, and he shall direct thy paths" (Proverbs 3:5-6).

Tomato and Pear were married 29 years. To God be the glory for their marriage. Their marriage had problems, ups and down, but God carried them through good times and bad times. "Happy is the man that findeth wisdom, and the man that getteth understanding" (Proverbs 3:13).

Two students were in college on a collision to meet from different towns. God order their steps. While visiting New York, he met this young lady who was very intelligent and an outstanding person. She also was a very energetic person who did not meet a stranger. He, too, was very gifted, knowledgeable, and a brilliant well-rounded person.

Fig and Lima Bean met at a friend's house in New York at a cookout. They were attracted to each other once they started talking to each other at the cookout. Two brilliant minds drawn together, Fig and Lima Bean could talk about a plethora of subjects including sports.

Lima Bean was playing basketball in New York. He really enjoyed playing the game. Lima Bean was a good player. He was loved by the New York people. Fig was a lawyer by trade. She, too, worked in New York.

Lima Bean and Fig met at cookout; they talked, and Lima Bean asked her out on a date. They went out on their first date. Fig and Lima Bean dated for about two years. After two years, Lima Bean asked her to marry him. Fig said yes to his proposal.

Fig set out to plan a wedding in another state. That was a big job to undertake, so she got some help from other family members to assist. Then they planned this gorgeous wedding. Finally, the wedding day was here, and they both were excited and happy. Lima Bean and Fig had beautiful wedding. "Wherefore they are no more twain, but one flesh. What therefore God hath joined together let not man put asunder" (Matthew 19:6).

Lima Bean and Fig went on their honeymoon in Jamaica. They were gone for one week on their honeymoon. Fig said she had a wonderful time with her husband. "Nevertheless, let everyone in particular so love his wife even as himself, and the wife see that she reverence her husband" (Ephesians 5:33).

Lima Bean and Fig had three children by birth and adoption. They really loved their children. In addition, they raised those children right. "He that spareth his rod hateth his son: but he that loveth him chasteneth him betimes" (Proverbs 13:24). Fig was a good wife and mother to her children. "Every wise woman buildeth her house: but the foolish plucketh it down with her hands" (Proverbs 14:1). They were married 23 years. "He that walketh in his uprightness feareth the Lord: but he that is perverse in his ways despiseth him" (Proverbs 14:2).

It was a beautiful November day, not very cold. The weather was just so calm. The mountain retreat was lovely, and we walked around and looked at the sights. My body and mind were just relaxing, thinking about nothing but enjoying the views. As we walked down the trail, we met this thick boisterous overexcited young man. We glanced at him and kept walking along the path.

When they got back to the lobby of the cabin, they saw him again. He walked over and introduced himself to them. "My name is Butter Bean," "and I am Mango," they said. He was in the military. He was vacationing in the mountains and staying in a cabin, too. They were all there for a Christian retreat from different churches. Even though he was in the military, Butter Bean came to the retreat on leave. They talked and exchanged phone numbers. They left the retreat and returned to their homes.

Butter Bean was stationed at Fort Trust in New York City. He lived a long way from Mango. They talked on the phone and decided to see each other on Butter Bean's next furlough. Mango was a woman who; "She openeth her mouth with wisdom; and in her tongue is the law of kindness" (Proverbs 31:26).

Butter Bean came to her hometown on furlough and stayed at the hotel. Mango went out on a date with him. They had a lovely dinner and went dancing. Mango went home for the night. Butter Bean did not tell her he was going overseas to Troy to defend the country. He would be gone for a year. He asked Mango to marry him when he returned from Troy. Therefore, Mango had a year to plan their wedding.

While Butter Bean was gone, Mango planned the wedding and they called each other and wrote letters. She involved him in all the wedding planning. Mango really missed seeing Butter Bean so much and could not wait for him to come back. They decided to have the wedding on the beach. A beach wedding would be so beautiful and special for the couple. Their family coming to the beach would make a family vacation out of their wedding time.

Butter Bean came back from Troy and was excited about getting married. Mango was glad he was back in the states. They went to Florida to get married on the beach. The wedding day came and all the family was there including the bride and groom. Butter Bean and Mango got marriage and spent their honeymoon in Florida, too. "Whoso findeth a wife findeth a good thing, and obtaineth favour of the lord" (Proverbs 18:22). They loved each other and were best friends and lovers. They continued to stay married and loved each other.

They had two children to their union, a girl and a boy. Their children grew into adulthood. The children turned out to be very nice young people and hard workers. Butter Bean and Mango raised them in the church. They have been married 40 years, still in love today. God is the head of their lives. "A wise man is strong; yea, a man of knowledge increaseth strength" (Proverbs 24:5). "Through wisdom is an house builded; and by understanding it is established" (Proverbs 24:3).

CONCLUSION

The *Guidepost to Marriage* is just what it says, rules to follow. Marriage guidelines will help us to do better with all kinds of situations. One of the first rules: "Be ye not unequally yoked together with unbelievers: for what fellowship hath righteousness with unrighteousness? and what communion hath light with darkness" (2 Corinthians 6:14)? Second rule: "The wife hath not power of her own body, but the husband: and likewise also the husband hath not power of his own body, but the wife" (1 Corinthians 7:4). Third rule: "Husbands, love your wives, even as Christ also loved the church, and gave himself for it;" (Ephesians 5:25) Fourth rule: "So ought men to love their wives as their own bodies. He that loveth his wife loveth himself" (Ephesians 5:28). Fifth rule: "And be ye kind one to another, tenderhearted, forgiving one another, even as God for Christ's sake hath forgiven you" (Ephesians 4:32). Following these guidelines should assist you in having a good marriage. Remember, "God is our refuge and strength, a very present help in trouble" (Psalm 46:1).

ABOUT THE AUTHOR

Dr. Brenda A. Holmes Thomas is a devoted child and servant of God who has dedicated her life to faith, family, and service to others. She is a retired educator who spent many years guiding and inspiring students through her work as a teacher.

Dr. Holmes Thomas enjoys traveling, singing, praising God, and meeting new people. Her life is richly blessed through her family. She is the proud mother of three biological children and four adopted children. She is also the loving grandmother of fourteen grandchildren—seven biological and seven adopted—and one great-grandchild.

Through *Guidepost to Marriage*, Dr. Holmes Thomas shares real-life experiences and biblical wisdom to encourage couples to follow God's Word as the foundation for a strong and successful marriage.

www.ingramcontent.com/pod-product-compliance
Lightning Source LLC
LaVergne TN
LVHW010945110826
845149LV00013B/2768

9798992715293